This revised edition published by Wayland in 2023

First published in 2008 by Wayland
Text copyright © Pat Thomas 2008
Illustrations copyright © Lesley Harker 2008

Wayland, an imprint of Hachette Children's Group
Part of Hodder and Stoughton
Carmelite House
50 Victoria Embankment
London EC4Y 0DZ

An Hachette UK Company
www.hachette.co.uk
www.hachettechildrens.co.uk

Printed and bound in China

Concept design: Sarah Finan
Series design: Paul Cherrill Creative Design
Consultant: Dr Kristina Routh

PB ISBN: 9781526323811
EBK ISBN: 9781526323866

MIX
Paper from
responsible sources
FSC® C104740
FSC
www.fsc.org

Why is it so Hard to Breathe?

A FIRST LOOK AT ASTHMA

Written by
PAT THOMAS

Illustrated by
LESLEY HARKER

WAYLAND

Would you like to know something amazing? You breathe air in and out of your lungs thousands of times a day.

Most of the time breathing is so easy that we never have to think about it. But for some people breathing can sometimes be really hard. These people have asthma.

When a really bad asthma attack
comes it can be frightening.

It can leave you coughing or wheezing
and gasping for air.

It may feel as if a giant is sitting on your chest stopping you from getting any air in.

What about you?
Have you ever found it hard to breathe?
What did it feel like?

Asthma is an illness that makes it hard to get
enough air into your lungs.

You can get it when you are an adult, but most people get it when they are young children.

Asthma is not like a cold – you can't catch it from someone.

And you can't always tell just by looking whether another person has asthma. Most of the time people with asthma breathe just like everyone else.

When you first find out you have asthma,
you can feel worried and will have
a lot of questions.

Your parents and your doctor can
help you to understand more about what
causes asthma and what you can do.

To check if you have asthma, a doctor might give you a test. He or she may ask you to blow one big puff into a special tube.

This tube measures how much air you can blow out all at once. People with asthma blow out less air than other people.

If your doctor thinks you have asthma,
he or she may also give you some other tests
to see if you have any allergies that might
cause your asthma.

Although asthma can't be cured, there are lots of ways to control it. Medicine is given in something called an inhaler.

With an inhaler you breathe medicine straight into your lungs.

Some inhalers are used in the morning
to prevent attacks during the day.

Some are carried around to make
it easier to breathe if you feel wheezy
during the day.

Lots of things can make asthma worse,
including allergies to things in the air.

dust

mould

smoke

pets' fur

feathers

traffic fumes

pollen

Cold weather and exercising without first
warming up your muscles also makes it worse.

Having a cold or being scared or unhappy
can also make asthma worse.

What about you?

Do you know anyone with asthma?

Do you know any of the things that
make their asthma worse?

People with asthma will learn to keep away from the things that make their asthma worse.

Sometimes it isn't possible to keep away from these things, so they can keep an inhaler with them in case.

Parents, teachers and friends can learn about what makes asthma worse so that they can help.

Asthma can be a pain. Sometimes it can make you feel as if you can't do the fun things everyone else does.

But people with asthma can do almost anything.

In fact, lots of famous sports people, singers
and people you see on TV have asthma.

They've learned that as long as they take a bit of extra care, having asthma doesn't mean they have to miss out on anything fun!

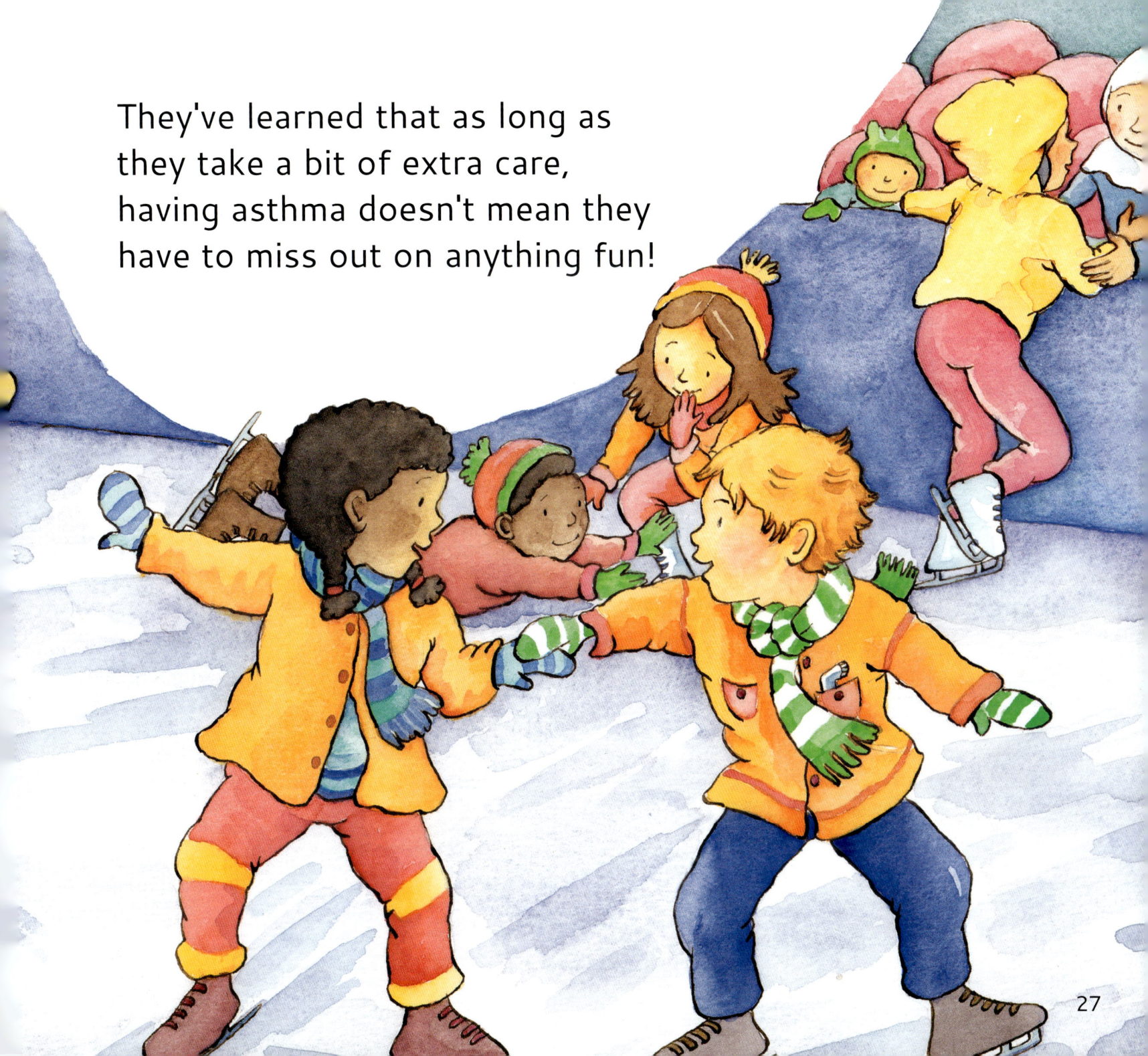

NOTES FOR PARENTS, CARERS AND TEACHERS

Whenever you talk to your child about health matters it's best to be honest, open and positive. Tell your child that asthma can't always be cured (only about half of children who have asthma 'grow out of it') but that medicine can help control the symptoms. Talk about the equipment your child may encounter such as peak flow monitors, nebulizers and different types of inhalers.

Be patient. Children in the four to seven age group will not fully understand their condition and cannot be expected to be in complete control of their environments in order to avoid all asthma triggers. At this age they will understand that they have lungs that help them breathe, that asthma makes breathing difficult and that certain things make asthma worse. But they may still expose themselves to triggers and risks if they are part of a group or if it looks like fun. Likewise they can understand and assist with medicines, but it is up to parents and other carers to provide help and supervision.

As early as you can, make sure your child learns to recognise the things that trigger an asthma attack and reinforce the need to avoid these things. With a slightly older child, it is worth exploring alternative breathing techniques such as those used in yoga or the Buteyko method. These can help your child breathe more fully and can help calm breathing when he or she feels an attack coming on.

Different children react to asthma differently. It's important to tailor your approach to your child and provide the right level of reassurance and empathy. As often as possible, help your child understand that while asthma can't be ignored, it doesn't mean that he or she can't live a normal life. You may wish to find out about famous people who have asthma and discuss these with your child to show them that what asthmatics do and achieve in life isn't limited by their disease. While your child is coming to terms with asthma, encourage descriptive, feeling words to describe symptoms.

Communication with carers and teachers is the key. If your child has asthma you will need to work with other adults who may care for him or her so that everyone knows what triggers to avoid and what to do if the child has an attack. Make sure you know of any activities that might impact your child's asthma. If you wish your child's health problems to remain confidential at school this should be respected.

In school, learning about asthma can be covered through health education (how the lungs work and what allergies are, for instance) and also through science (e.g. understanding environmental triggers such as pollen). Many pupils may have experience of asthma: they may have it themselves, or have a family member with asthma, or a friend may have the condition.

An interesting way to get children who don't have asthma to understand what it feels like is to stage a simple exercise. Have the children run in place for one minute. They should be breathing hard and fast when they finish. When they stop, tell them to block their noses, put a straw in their mouths and close their lips around it, and then try to breathe through the straw (they should only do this for a few seconds). This will give them an indication of how hard it can be to get air into the lungs when the airways have closed up.

FURTHER READING

All About Asthma by Megan Boghert–Spaniol
(Super Sandcastle, 2018)

I Have Asthma, What Does That Mean?
by Wendy Chen and Izzy Bean (Wendy Chen books, 2015)

Roo with Asthma: how to handle an asthma attack
by Abraham Thomas (Kids Medical Books, 2021)

RESOURCES

Asthma UK
www.asthma.org.uk
Lots of advice about what asthma is and how to
effectively manage it. They also do a 3–minute
asthma attack risk checker test.
Helpline: 0300 222 5800

Allergy UK
www.allergyuk.org
Supporting people living with allergies
Helpline: 01322 619898

Beat Asthma
www.beatasthma.co.uk/resources/young–
people–with–asthma/
Advice and support for children with asthma

British Lung Foundation
www.lunguk.org
Advice about good breathing techniques